GREEK BEASTS AND HEROES

The Magic Head

You can read the stories in the
Greek Beasts and Heroes series in any order.

If you'd like to read more about some of
the characters in this book, turn to pages 78 and 79
to find out which other books to try.

Atticus's journey began in
The Beasts in the Jar, and continues in ...

GREEK BEASTS AND HEROES

The Magic Head

LUCY COATS

Illustrated by Anthony Lewis

Orion
Children's Books

Text and illustrations first appeared in
Atticus the Storyteller's 100 Greek Myths
First published in Great Britain in 2002
by Orion Children's Books
This edition published in Great Britain in 2010
by Orion Children's Books
a division of the Orion Publishing Group Ltd
Orion House
5 Upper St Martin's Lane
London WC2H 9EA
An Hachette UK company

3 5 7 9 8 6 4 2

The Orion Publishing Group's policy is to use papers that are natural,
renewable and recyclable products and made from wood grown in sustainable
forests. The logging and manufacturing processes are expected to conform
to the environmental regulations of the country of origin.

A catalogue record for this book is available from the British Library

ISBN 978 1 4440 0066 5

Printed in China

www.orionbooks.co.uk
www.lucycoats.com

For Cat, Laurence, Charlie, Frannie,
Prisca and all my "greats" from
the Tante Ancienne with love.
L. C.

For the children and staff of
Manley & Mouldsworth Pre-school
A. L.

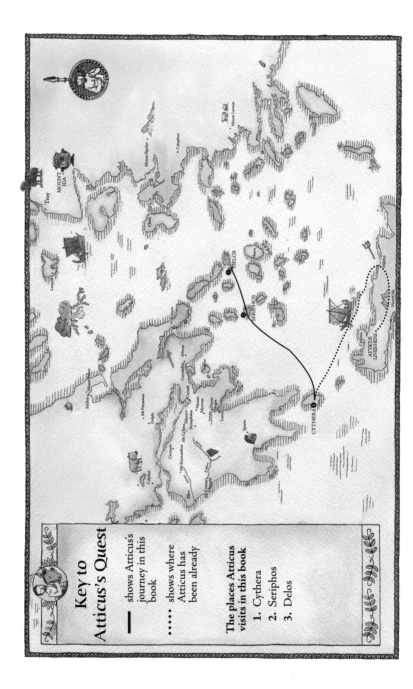

Key to Atticus's Quest

— shows Atticus's journey in this book

····· shows where Atticus has been already

The places Atticus visits in this book

1. Cythera
2. Seriphos
3. Delos

Contents

Stories from the Heavens

Long ago, in ancient Greece, gods and goddesses, heroes and heroines lived together with fearful monsters and every kind of

fabulous beast that ever flew, or walked or swam. But little by little, as people began to build more villages and towns and cities, the gods and monsters disappeared into the secret places of the world and the heavens, so that they could have some peace.

 9

Before they disappeared,
the gods and goddesses
gave the gift of storytelling
to men and women, so that
nobody would ever forget them. They
ordered that there should be a great
storytelling festival once every seven years
on the slopes of Mount Ida, near Troy,
and that tellers of tales should come
from all over Greece and from lands near
and far to take part. Every seven years a

 beautiful painted vase,
filled to the brim with gold,
magically appeared as a first
prize, and the winner was
honoured for the rest of his

life by all the people of Greece.

It was late autumn, and Atticus and Melissa the donkey were on the long journey from their home in Crete to the Storytelling Festival at Troy.

They had landed on the island of Cythera two days before, and were travelling slowly north, when huge towers of black clouds appeared on the horizon. Atticus and Melissa hurried to take shelter under some great rocks as thunder and lightning flashed and roared over the sea.

"This is just like the thunderstorm Zeus found himself in once," said Atticus. "I think I'd better tell you about it while we're waiting for this to blow over."

The Cuckoo's Trick

Zeus was brave, he was strong, he was handsome – in fact he was the greatest of the gods. So why wouldn't beautiful Hera marry him?

He brought her magical flowers that bloomed a different colour each day. He brought her crowns made of moon-beams and necklaces made of starlight.

But Hera just looked down her long, straight, perfect nose and laughed.

"Oh Zeus!" she sighed. "Just leave me alone and go and play with your thunder-bolts. I'll never marry you until you can sit on my lap without me noticing – and that will be never!"

 12

And Zeus stomped back to his palace in a terrible temper that made the earth below shake and tremble.

Then he had an idea. He would do just what Hera had told him. He would go and play with his thunderbolts. Zeus stirred up the most tremendous thunderstorm that ever was. Then he changed himself into a cuckoo, and set out for Hera's palace through the storm. Wet, bedraggled and exhausted, he flew through the window of her bedroom, and landed shaking on her bed.

"Poor little cuckoo!" said Hera, stroking his soaking grey feathers. "Let me dry you."

In no time at all the cuckoo was dry and comfortable, and nestling into Hera's lap.

Then the cuckoo began to change. It grew and grew until – there was Zeus sitting in Hera's lap, laughing.

"Cuckoo!" he said, kissing her. "Will you marry me now?"

And Hera had to agree.

Zeus and Hera were given many amazing wedding

presents by all the gods and goddesses in celebration of their marriage.

The most wonderful of all was the magical apple tree given to Hera by Mother Earth. Its fruit was as golden as the sun, and it gave everlasting life to anyone who ate it.

Hera planted it in her special garden, and set three beautiful nymphs to guard it, together with Argos, the hundred-eyed monster who never slept.

In later times Heracles, the bravest hero of all, stole some of the precious apples, but that is quite another story.

When the storm was over Atticus pulled his wet cloak more closely around his shoulders as they walked northwards.

"Winter will soon be here, Melissa," he said. "I smell frost."

Melissa flattened her ears and shivered. The flowers on the hillsides of Cythera were all dying now, and fluffy seed puffs blew across the path as they walked towards the sea.

"This time of year reminds me of Demeter, looking for her beautiful daughter all over the earth."

And he began the story.

The Queen of the Underworld

Demeter, goddess of the harvest, had hair the colour of sunset, and lips and cheeks as pink and perfect as a summer morning.

Wherever she walked on the earth, trees would burst into fruit, and corn ripen to burning gold; flowers would waft sweet scents towards her, and vegetables swell and pop with green juicy life.

She had a daughter called Kore, the most lovely child ever born, and it was Demeter's delight to play with her all the long sunny days of summer – and where Demeter was it was always summer.

 17

But when Kore was about sixteen years old, she was seen picking flowers in the fields and woods by Hades, the dark god of the Underworld.

Hades fell in love with her at once, but he knew that Demeter would never give permission for him to marry her – he would have to kidnap her instead.

So one bright afternoon Hades drove his chariot pulled by six black horses out of a huge crack in the ground, seized Kore in his arms, and carried her off screaming to his kingdom of Tartarus,

deep in the Underworld. Only a little
shepherd boy and his brother had seen
what had happened and they were
too scared to say anything.

For a whole year Demeter travelled
in search of her daughter, calling and
calling. And while she called, tears ran
down her face so fast that it became all
wrinkled and crinkled, and her lovely hair
turned grey and lank with sadness.

Nothing grew or bloomed any more, and the earth became a frozen, dark place, where the North Wind blew snow and ice over the fields, and no birds sang. Men, women and children shivered and shook as they huddled round their fires and starved.

In the heavens, only Helios the sun god had seen what Hades had done. He

told Zeus, but as usual, Zeus decided not to interfere with his dark brother's doings.

However, he soon noticed how cold and unhappy the mortals on earth were. There were no nice-smelling sacrifices to the gods, no prayers, only misery.

He saw at once that he would have to do something after all, and so he sent his messenger, Hermes, to comfort Demeter.

"Don't you worry, my dear. I'll get her back for you," said Hermes, who had just talked to the two shepherd boys and found out where Kore was.

And down he went to visit Hades, down, down, down to Tartarus in the deepest part of the earth, where the dead souls of men and heroes wander like mist.

Now it is well known that if you eat any food from the Underworld, you can never return to the earth.

21

Kore knew this, and so although Hades had tempted her with delicious food and drink, she had not touched a single morsel in all the time she had been there.

All she had eaten was three seeds from a pomegranate growing in Hades' garden, when she thought nobody was looking.

When Hermes came to demand that Kore be returned to her mother, Hades smiled a nasty smile.

"Little Kore has been very silly!" he smirked. "She thought nobody would see her. But my gardener was hiding behind a tree, and he swears he saw her spit three pomegranate pips into a bush!"

Kore burst into tears. Now she would never escape from her dreary prison, where the sun never shone, and the only birdsong was the cawing of ravens.

But Hermes was very crafty.

"If you don't send Kore back to Demeter, everyone on earth will die from cold and starvation, and you will be so busy sorting the dead souls out that you won't have time to even think, let alone enjoy yourself. Why don't you let her spend a month here for every seed she ate, and the rest with her mother up on the earth?"

Hades knew when he was beaten, and he agreed to Hermes' plan. So Kore went back to her mother for nine months of the year, and the earth bloomed once more.

 23

But for the three months that we call winter, Kore now changes her name to Persephone, and goes to live with Hades underground. And the cold winds blow, and the snow falls, and Demeter weeps tears of ice because she misses her daughter so much.

They reached the sea and Melissa trotted
happily along the sand behind Atticus.
The sun was coming up, it was a beautiful
crisp day and her coat was dry again.

"This is where Aphrodite was born,"
said Atticus, sitting down on a rock to rest,
and picking up a piece of green seaweed.
"It was like this."

The Foam Goddess

Many years ago, when Uranus fled into the deepest heavens, one drop of blood from the great wound that his son, Cronus, had given him dripped into the sea and changed into foam.

"We must not waste this precious gift," whispered the waves.

And they rushed at the magic foam, and swirled it and whirled it into the shape of the most beautiful goddess of all, Aphrodite.

A giant scallop shell was brought up from the depths of the ocean on the back of a whale, and six dolphins were harnessed to it.

Then Aphrodite stepped into it and settled onto its pink velvety cushions while she was blown to the shores of the island of Cythera by the West Wind.

As she stepped onto the earth for the first time, clouds of sparrows and doves flew twittering and cooing round her head, and three lovely maidens brought her robes made of sea-spray and rainbows.

When Zeus saw her exquisite beauty, he knew that all the gods would fight over her, so he quickly married her off to his son, the lame blacksmith god Hephaestus.

"That will keep her out of trouble," he thought to himself.

Aphrodite was not at all happy about this, for Hephaestus was always black and sooty from the dirt of his forge fires.

"Ugh! Get off!" she snarled, as he kissed her on their wedding night. "Look at your dirty fingerprints all over my clean robe!"

She would much rather have married his brother, handsome Ares, or funny Hermes who teased her and made her laugh. But Aphrodite soon came round when she saw the beautiful things that Hephaestus made for her.

The most wonderful of all was a magic golden girdle, set with glittering jewels.

29

Whenever Aphrodite wore it, she was so lovely that no one could resist anything she asked, not even if it was Zeus himself.

Although she lived on Olympus, Aphrodite always went back to her birthplace for a month's holiday every year. And when she came back to her palace, the very flowers bowed beneath her feet in amazement at her shining beauty and grace.

She had a little son called Eros whom she thought was the most beautiful child in the world. Together they danced across the earth and the heavens shooting gods and mortals alike with their arrows of love, and as they passed, even the cold hearts of the stars were filled with joy.

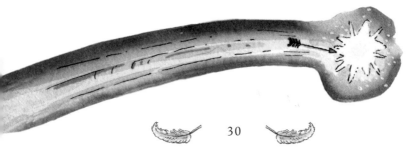

Atticus was hot and bothered. He and Melissa had nearly missed the boat from Cythera to Seriphos, and now he was sitting squashed up against some bales of cloth with Melissa beside him.

The sea was rough and it was raining. A sailor with a wooden leg was steering a wobbly course past the tip of the mainland.

"He reminds me of the blacksmith god Hephaestus," whispered Atticus in Melissa's ear. "And he's certainly dirty enough to be a smith! I'll tell you the story very quietly, so as not to annoy him."

The Lame Blacksmith

Hephaestus was the son of Zeus and Hera. As a baby, he was rather small and puny, and he didn't like loud noises. So when his father threw thunderbolts, and his mother shouted, he cowered in his cradle and shivered. As a little boy, though, he grew braver, and one day when his parents were arguing, he tried to stop them.

"You hurt my ears!" he said, glaring at Zeus. "Why don't you both just stop shouting – **Yack! Bang! Yell! Yack! Bang! Yell!** – I'm fed up with listening to you." Now this made Zeus so angry that he picked Hephaestus up by his ears and flung him down to earth.

Hephaestus fell for a whole day, and when he landed feet first on the island of Lemnos, his leg bones shattered into tiny pieces, and he fainted from the pain. There, Thetis the sea-nymph found him, and carried him to her cave, where she and her daughter looked after him for nine whole years.

 33

Because Hephaestus was now lame, and couldn't get around easily, he amused himself by making beautiful things with his strong hands, and soon he was the cleverest smith and jeweller that ever lived.

One day Hera met Thetis at a party, and admired her dolphin brooch, made of sea pearls and sapphires.

"Where did you get that?" she asked. "I must have one myself!"

When she discovered that it was her own son who was the craftsman, she carried him straight to Olympus and made Zeus apologise and set him up as official blacksmith to the gods.

Zeus was very sorry for what he had done, and that was why he chose Hephaestus to be Aphrodite's husband.

Hephaestus built a smithy deep in

the heart of the mountains, with twenty bellows worked by the Cyclopes, who became his assistants.

Among the amazing things he made were two robots of silver and gold, which would do anything he asked.

And when the gods had meetings, they used his little magic tables, which ran around on golden wheels, taking food and drink to anyone who needed it.

It was still raining, and the boat to Seriphos was crowded with goods, people and animals. Atticus kept pushing an inquisitive pig away from him.

"This cloth must be going to Tyre to be dyed," he said to the man with the pig. "I'd love a Tyrrhenian blue cloak, but they're so expensive."

The pig's owner grunted. "Wish this boat would hurry up," he said. "I hate the sea."

"Would you like me to tell you a story to pass the time?" Atticus asked.

The pig man grunted again. "Go on then!" He closed his eyes as Atticus began.

The Bull from the Sea

Zeus loved his birthplace, Crete. He knew every rocky inch of it, the way the hills smelled of thyme in the sunshine, the way the dark sea sounded when it rushed against the shore. He knew the little white villages, and the narrow ledges where the seagulls nested, and the caves where bats hung from dark crevices in the stone.

"Crete needs a queen," he thought one day, as he flew back to Olympus.

"But where can I find a woman good and beautiful enough to take care of my beloved island for me?"

Zeus looked and looked whenever he visited earth. But every woman he saw was either too tall or too short, too fat or too thin, too chatty or too silent.

Not one woman came close to what he wanted until one day, flying over the city of Tyre, he saw a girl playing on the seashore with some of her friends.

"Ha!" said Zeus, making himself invisible. "This is the one. She's perfect!"

Europa was the King of Tyre's daughter. She had long, dark hair as shiny as chestnuts, and grey eyes that turned as blue as dye when she was happy. They were blue now, but they quickly changed back to grey as she looked at the sea and saw a great white bull wading up towards her out of the waves.

At first, Europa and her friends were frightened, but when the bull lay down quietly on the shore and looked at them through his long silky eyelashes, they came closer and stroked his furry flanks.

The bull snorted softly, and his breath smelled of violets.

"Ooh, isn't he sweet?" squealed Europa. "Do let's make some garlands for his horns, and then we can take him back to the palace and keep him as a pet!"

So the girls ran into the meadows by the beach and picked some sea pinks and cistus and wove them into garlands. Europa was the tallest, so she climbed onto the bull's broad back to slip them over his sharp horns.

As she knelt astride his shoulders, the bull got up and started to gallop out to sea along a great road of shining water that had suddenly appeared.

Europa's friends screamed and ran after him into the waves, but it was no good – the bull had vanished as quickly as he had come.

Europa was a brave girl, so she was not a bit surprised when the bull spoke to her as he ran.

"I am Zeus, greatest of the gods," he bellowed. "I have chosen you to be Queen

of Crete. I shall marry you as my mortal wife, and we will have fine sons together."

And what Zeus said came true. After he had married Europa, and given her a crown of beautiful jewels, they had three strong sons.

Europa ruled happily in the palace Zeus built for her, and she was helped by a marvellous bronze robot called Talos, which Hephaestus had made for her on Zeus's orders.

Talos clanked around the island on his metal legs three times a day, and if an enemy ship came near, he threw rocks at it.

Together, Talos and Europa kept Crete safe from any enemies for many long years.

It was a great relief when they landed on the island of Seriphos.

"Pooh!" said Atticus. "That pig was smelly. I need a wash!"

Melissa wrinkled her nose and trotted on fast towards a little spring by the roadside.

Atticus washed his hands and face and sat down. "This is where the hero Perseus was brought up," he said. "I'll tell you the story."

The Copper Tower

King Acrisius of Argos was the most superstitious man in the world.

He saw omens in the moon and stars; if his ships needed wind for their sails he whistled for it, and if he walked under a ladder, he stayed in bed for a week to avoid bad luck.

Now Acrisius had a daughter called Danäe, who was the apple of his eye. "Hello, my flower!" he would say every morning. "Come and give your old father a kiss."

But when Danäe was about seventeen, a soothsayer came to Argos, and demanded to tell the king's fortune. He was rather grubby, with a hat hung with rats' tails and a necklace of wild animal teeth.

 45

The king was just about to offer him a goblet of wine, and ask what he could do for him, when the soothsayer swayed in front of him and started to dribble and foam at the mouth.

"Beware, oh King, beware!" he wailed. "For your flower will give birth to a seed, and when the seed is grown, then you will die!"

And with that, he turned and ran from the room as fast as a leopard.

Acrisius was horrified, but it was quite obvious what the man had meant. So he shut Danäe up in a tower which he covered from top to bottom in copper, so that no one could get in or out.

Only a small flap at the foot for food and a small hole in the roof for air were left, and no one could have got through those.

"Now she will never have children," said the king. "And I shall live for ever!"

But Zeus was passing by as Acrisius spoke, and the king's words made him very angry.

"We shall see about that," he roared in Acrisius's frightened ear. "For only the gods can make you immortal, and I don't think you deserve it!"

And with that he changed himself into a shower of golden rain and dived through the hole in the roof of Danäe's tower.

Danäe was very pleased to see the pretty raindrops, and they danced and played with her all day long.

In due course, Danäe gave birth to a baby boy called Perseus, but Danäe always thought of him as her little rainbow.

Acrisius didn't dare to offend Zeus by harming his grandchild, because he knew that Perseus was Zeus's son. But he knew he had to get rid of him.

So at dead of night he and his soldiers made a big hole in the tower, and dragged Perseus and Danäe out. They were bundled into a large chest, and thrown off the harbour wall into the sea below.

"That way," thought Acrisius, "if anything bad happens I can blame it on Poseidon." And he went back to his palace and climbed into bed.

The chest tossed and tumbled through the waves at first. But Zeus sent some nymphs to carry it through the sea, and soon the chest bumped up against the shores of Seriphos. A very wet Danäe, clutching a cold and crying baby, climbed out onto the shore of the island.

Just then, a poor shepherd passed by, and saw her standing there shivering. He took off his cloak and wrapped her and Perseus in it.

Then he took them back to his cottage, and they lived there happily for many years until Perseus grew up into a handsome young man and went off on his adventures.

After a rest, Atticus and Melissa set off again. Soon they passed through a village.

"Hey! Where are you going?" yelled a boy, running after them.

"I'm off to catch the boat for Delos. Would you like to walk with me for a bit? I'll tell you a story."

"A story? With monsters?" said the boy.

Atticus laughed and held out his hand. "What's your name?" he asked.

"Perseus. My father's the blacksmith."

"Well, Perseus, I'll tell you the story of another brave boy called Perseus – one who fought a real monster. And like you, he lived right here on Seriphos!"

The Snake-Haired Gorgon

The king of Seriphos wanted to marry Princess Danäe, but she didn't want to marry him at all. So Perseus, Danäe's son by Zeus, went to the king and asked him to find someone else to marry. The king pretended to agree, but what he really wanted was to get Perseus out of the way.

"I suppose I could marry another princess," he said. "But you will have to go off and do some very difficult task to make up for my disappointment."

Perseus would have done anything to save his mother, and he said so.

"Very well," said the king nastily. "You shall go and kill the Gorgon Medusa for me."

"Never mind, mother!" said Perseus as he told Danäe the news. "Surely this old Gorgon can't be too hard to kill. I'll just sneak up on her somehow, and chop her head off while she isn't looking."

But Danäe just wailed harder. In fact she wailed so hard that Zeus himself heard her, and looked down from Olympus.

Now Zeus didn't like the king of Seriphos, and because Perseus was his own son, he decided to give him some help.

As Perseus set out on his journey, leaving his weeping mother behind, two shining figures appeared on the road in front of him.

"Hail, Perseus!" said the first, a beautiful woman with an owl on her shoulder. "I am Athene."

And she gave him a magic shield, all polished like a mirror.

"Hail, Perseus!" said the second, a cheeky-looking youth with a winged hat on his curly head, and winged sandals on his feet. "I am Hermes."

And he handed Perseus a magical sword with words engraved on its blade.

HARD AS A DIAMOND
THOUGH IT BE, THE HARDEST
THING CAN BE CUT BY ME!

"These will help you against the Gorgon Medusa," said Hermes. "But you need three more magical things if you are to succeed, and they are held by the Nymphs of the North. The only people who know where their house is are the Three Grey Women, who are Medusa's sisters. If you come with me, and do just as I say, I can trick them into telling you the way."

Perseus was so amazed by his good luck that he just stood there with his mouth open.

Hermes took his hand, and away they flew together, up, up, up into the blue sky, on, on, on till the earth changed to white beneath them and the clouds turned dark and sulky above.

The Three Grey Women were quarrelling when Perseus and Hermes landed behind their hut at dusk.

 55

"It's my turn!" shrieked the eldest, who was thin and wispy with long, tangled hair and fingernails like rusty swords.

"No! Mine!" screeched the middle sister, who was dumpy and bedraggled, with ears like slimy grey slugs.

"You can't have them till tomorrow!" hissed the youngest, who was completely bald, with a nose like a vulture's beak.

"They only have one eye and one tooth between them," whispered Hermes, "and they're always fighting over them. Now, while I distract the Grey Women, you go and snatch them, and then we can bargain."

He stepped out from behind the hut.

"Good morning!" said Hermes, grinning. And he produced a long feather from behind his back and began to tickle the sisters all over.

They laughed so much that the eye and tooth fell out of the youngest one's grasp, and rolled towards Perseus, who picked them up and put them in his pocket.

"Time for business!" said Hermes. "Where are the Nymphs of the North?"

"WE'LL NEVER TELL YOU!" yelled the sisters.

Hermes sighed. "Then we'll just have to drop your eye and tooth in the sea," he said.

There was dead silence and then all three sisters began babbling.

"Left at the ash tree . . . straight on till Dragon Mountain . . . past the Sea of Serpents and it's first on the right."

"Thank you!" said Hermes, soaring into the air with Perseus. "Now catch!"

And he took the eye and tooth from Perseus and threw them to the ground. The shrieks and curses followed them for miles.

The Nymphs of the North welcomed Perseus, and gladly gave him the magical leather bag, winged sandals and cap of invisibility which he needed.

"Where are you?" asked Hermes, after he had put them on.

"Up here!" laughed the invisible Perseus from above the treetops. And off he flew to look for Medusa, with Hermes's last words floating up to him.

"Use your shield as a mirror to look at the Gorgons, or you will be turned to stone! And remember, Medusa is the only one that looks human!"

After flying for a very long way, he saw a rocky little island thousands of feet below.

There was a beach of snowy white sand on the far side, and fast asleep by a cave in the cliffs lay three monsters. They were covered in gigantic greeny-bronze insect scales, and their long,

thin, golden wings rose and fell as they breathed. Instead of hair they all had snakes growing from their heads, writhing and hissing as they slept.

Perseus looked at them carefully in his shield mirror.

Which was Medusa?

As the monsters sighed and turned over, he saw that the nearest had the face of a beautiful woman.

Perseus landed softly and raised his sword, taking careful aim in the mirror. The sword snickered through the silent air and cut down to the sand beneath, as Medusa's head rolled off her shoulders and landed with a thump at his feet.

Quickly he opened the magic bag, which stretched itself to the right size at once, and stuffed Medusa's head inside. He felt the snakes wriggling as he attached it to his belt and flew towards the sun.

At that moment the other Gorgons
woke up and found their sister dead.
How their talons clawed and scratched
the air as they flapped round the island,
shrieking horribly and looking for
someone to turn to stone.

But the invisible Perseus fled
hurriedly in the other direction, the
Gorgon's head safe at his side.

At dawn the next day, Atticus and Melissa left Seriphos and boarded the boat for Delos. Atticus was pleased at how well the journey was going, although it would be months before they reached Troy.

"That's the way Perseus flew when he'd killed Medusa," he said to Melissa, pointing to the south-east. "There was a terrible storm, and he got blown off course."

"Sounds like a good story for a sailor," said Captain Nikos, who owned the boat.

So Atticus told the tale while Captain Nikos steered *The Star of the Sea* towards Delos.

The Magic Head

The wind blew and the lightning flashed, and Perseus was blown this way and that, through thunder and clouds and rain, till he didn't know which way was up. He clutched his precious bag with one hand and his cap of invisibility with the other, and prayed to Zeus to save him.

But Zeus had sent the storm on purpose.

As soon as Perseus was over the coast of Ethiopia, the wind died, and the sun came out in a sky as blue as delphiniums. Looking down, he saw a great rock. Something was moving on the top of it, and Perseus flew down to have a closer look. There, chained to a post, was the loveliest girl he had ever seen.

"Who are you, and what are you doing here?" he asked as he landed, and took off his cap.

The girl screamed as he appeared, but when he had calmed her down, she told him that she was Andromeda, the daughter of the king and queen, and that she had been left as a sacrifice to Poseidon, the god of the sea, whom her mother had offended.

"Run for your life," she said. "A monster is coming to eat me up, and if you stay here you will be killed as well!"

But Perseus had fallen in love with Andromeda, and was determined to save her if he could.

 65

So he hid behind a rock and waited.

Soon a great roiling and boiling in the sea started, and a huge warty head appeared, with trails of seaweed and slime hanging from it.

The monster opened its mouth, and showed its teeth, each one as long as a man's arm.

As Andromeda cowered away, Perseus ran forward with his magic sword and plunged it into the creature's throat. It nearly bit his arm off as it reared away, roaring and pouring blood into the water.

With the monster dead, Perseus cut through Andromeda's chains, and they flew to her father's palace. The king and queen were surprised and delighted to see their daughter alive, and agreed that Perseus could marry her at once.

But just then in came the man who had been engaged to Andromeda before she had gone off to be sacrificed. He was furious at the king and queen's decision, and rushed at Perseus with his sword raised.

Perseus whipped Medusa's head out of his bag, and in a trice the man was turned to stone.

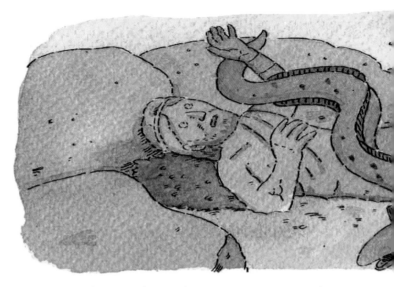

Andromeda and Perseus returned
to Seriphos, but Danäe was nowhere to
be found. The king of Seriphos had tried
to marry her again, and she had gone
into hiding.

"How dare he annoy my
mother!" roared Perseus.

And he marched into the throne
room and thrust Medusa's head into
the king's surprised face, turning him
to stone at once.

The people of Seriphos were happy,

 68

because the king had been cruel to all
of them. His stone body was thrown
into the harbour, and Perseus and
Andromeda were crowned king and
queen in his place.

Danäe came out of hiding, and the
joyful hugging and feasting and laughter
went on for weeks and weeks. Perseus
soon gave Medusa's head and the other
magical things back to the gods.

And he was so happy that he vowed
never to go on any adventures again.

Atticus waved goodbye to Captain Nikos. "See you on the other side of Delos," he called as he stopped at a little market stall by the harbour. A woman was weighing out olives while a boy and a girl were hanging onto her legs and screaming.

"Stories?" she asked. "I wish you'd take these two off my hands for an hour and tell them a story so I could get some work done!"

"I will," said Atticus, "if you'll give me some olives, and some cheese and a bit of bread."

Atticus and the children sat under a shady olive tree, munching and spitting out stones. Atticus stretched and yawned.

"See those sunbeams?" he asked. "Those are what Apollo's arrows are made from."

The children wriggled closer and settled down to listen.

Black Python and the Arrows of the Sun

Long ago, when the world was new and strange, Poseidon created the floating island of Delos. It was shaped like a sock, and completely bare except for one huge palm tree right in the middle.

One day, the goddess Leto landed on the island, right under the palm tree, panting and shaking with fear.

"Hide me quickly, island of the palm tree!" she whispered. "Hera is angry with me! She has sent a terrible snake after me, and she has forbidden the earth to let me step on her body. But you are not attached to the earth, so perhaps I will be safe here!"

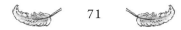

Now the reason Hera was so cross with Leto was because Zeus had fallen in love with her, and that made Hera very jealous. Even worse, Leto was going to have twins, and Hera was determined they should not be born, but should stay inside their mother for ever and ever.

Zeus loved Hera even though he was sometimes a bit afraid of her, and he knew he had done wrong, but he also loved Leto.

So he persuaded the other goddesses to invite Hera to a party and give her a most beautiful necklace with jewels that gave off a light like sunshine through leaves.

Hera was so distracted by the necklace that she forgot about Leto, and soon the babies were born – a boy and a girl named Apollo and Artemis.

Zeus was pleased with his lovely twins, and he gave them each a magical quiver of arrows and a bow to go with them. Artemis's were as soft as the rays of the moon, and Apollo's were as sharp as sunlight.

And after they were born, he fixed the island of Delos to the earth, and covered it with trees and flowers and made sandy crescent-shaped coves along its shores so that his children should grow up with beauty all around them.

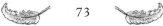

Now the snake that Hera had sent to kill Leto lived at a place called Delphi. Her name was Python, and she was black and shiny, with needle-sharp fangs that dripped poison and slime. She was also very clever, because she was an oracle and could see into the future. People used to come from far and wide to ask her advice.

Delphi had once been a beautiful wooded slope where nymphs sang and played, but Python had made it into a frightening place, full of echoes and shadows and whispers of grey mist.

She lived in a damp dark drippy cave, full of bats and spiders, and her throne was a great rock covered in black moss, with a magic pool beneath it, in which Python saw visions of what would happen.

Zeus wanted to get rid of Python, because she had once been rude to him, so when Apollo grew up, he sent him off in a great silver chariot pulled by ice-white swans.

"Kill her with the arrows I gave you," he told Apollo. "She doesn't like bright light."

Apollo landed his swans and crept up the hill towards Python's cave. But as he set foot outside her cave, he heard a great hiss.

"Welcome, ssson of Zeusss!
My magic pool told me you would come!
Come closer sssoo I can ssseee you.
Look into my eyessss!"

In two shakes of a snake's tail, Apollo found himself inside the mouth of the cave, staring into a pair of eyes like polished black glass.

"*Closser, closssser!*" hissed the snake.

Just then, Apollo trod on something that crunched, and looked down.

Python's fangs just missed his ear, and he jumped back, drawing his bow, and fitting an arrow to the string as he went.

The cave blazed with light, and the great snake screamed, thrashing her tail so wildly that Apollo was knocked off his feet.

The arrow had landed right between Python's eyes, and as she died, her spirit fled down to the Underworld, where she hissed the names of those who were to die each day into Hades' ear.

Now that Python was defeated, the nymphs came back to Delphi once more, and made it a place of light and music.

And Apollo built a temple around the magic pool and put his own priestess there so that people can visit to hear the Delphic oracle tell their future to this very day.

Greek Beasts and Heroes and where to find them ...

 So why did Heracles steal Hera's precious apples? You can read all about it in *The Flying Horse* – just look for the story called 'The Golden Apples'.

 Hera's garden was protected by three lovely nymphs and a hundred-eyed watchman monster called Argos. His story is told in *The Silver Chariot*.

Aphrodite "The Foam Goddess" was created from a single drop of Uranus's blood. Find out what happened to the three other magic blood droplets in "The Kindly Ones" (who weren't nearly as nice as Aphrodite!). Look for that one in *The Silver Chariot* too.

Everyone loves Aphrodite – she is even woven into a special tapestry picture when boastful Arachne and the goddess Athene take part in a fast and furious weaving contest. Find out who wins in "The Web Spinner", which is told in *The Monster in the Maze*.

Perseus was strong and brave when he fought Medusa. His famous great-grandson Heracles was even stronger and braver! Follow some of his exciting adventures in *The Fire Breather*.

Someone stole Apollo's cows – but who? Find out in *The Silver Chariot*. And if you'd like to know even more about Apollo, meet him again in *The Monster in the Maze*. Look for the story called "The Girl Who Grew into a Bay Tree".